'It's tear gas with just a hint of burning Peugeot'

THE BEST OF

MATT

2019

MATTHEW PRITCHETT
studied at St Martin's School of Art in
London and first saw himself published
in the *New Statesman* during one of its rare
lapses from high seriousness. He has been
the *Daily Telegraph*'s front-page pocket
cartoonist since 1988. In 1995, 1996, 1999,
2005, 2009 and 2013 he was the winner of
the Cartoon Arts Trust Award and in 1991,
2004 and 2006 he was 'What the Papers
Say' Cartoonist of the Year. In 1996, 1998,
2000, 2008, 2009 and 2018 he was the
UK Press Cartoonist of the Year and in 2015
he was awarded the Journalists' Charity
Award. In 2002 he received an MBE.

Own your favourite Matt cartoons.
Browse the full range of Matt
cartoons and buy online at
www.telegraph.co.uk/mattprints
or call 0191 6030178.

'We told the homeowner that we'd caught the burglar and the shock proved too much for him'

The Daily Telegraph

THE BEST OF

MATT

2019

ORION

An Orion Paperback

First published in Great Britain in 2019 by Orion Books
A division of the Orion Publishing Group Ltd
Carmelite House
50 Victoria Embankment
London
EC4Y 0DZ

A Hachette UK Company

10 9 8 7 6 5 4 3 2 1

A CIP catalogue record for this book is available from the British Library.

ISBN: 978 1 4091 6467 8

Printed and bound by CPI Group (UK) Ltd, Croydon, CR0 4YY

The Orion Publishing Group's policy is to use papers that are natural,
renewable and recyclable products and made from wood grown in
sustainable forests. The logging and manufacturing processes are
expected to conform to the environmental regulations of the country
of origin.

www.orionbooks.co.uk

'Apparently, after a no-deal Brexit, the only survivors will be cockroaches'

'When books are written
about this, remind me not
to read any of them'

'Brexit means Brexit'

'Now remove the Irish
backstop from the
Withdrawal Agreement'

'I'd like to join the Euro army.
There's a Brexit deal
I'm trying to forget'

'If I'd known house prices would fall 35pc after Brexit I'd have voted for it'

'If we can't work out how to leave, no cheese becomes a very real possibility'

'Let in any highly-skilled migrants. Particularly if they have a Brexit plan'

'MPs' holidays have been cancelled. That tin can won't kick itself down the road'

'If Theresa May was in charge of Boris's divorce he'd end up still married'

'I voted Leave to stop the
free movement of
vacuum cleaners'

'We solved the mystery. That
whining sound is coming
from Government ministers'

Production moves abroad

'This refers to the number of
Mars bars the UK will have
after a no-deal Brexit'

'It's the Bank of England's
Christmas jumper'

'I'm stockpiling myrrh
in case there's a
no-deal Brexit'

'If it was up to me, I'd choose
to crash out of the EU
with no deal'

'Give a man a fish and he'll
eat for a day. Teach a man
to fish and he'll receive £6bn
in no-deal Brexit support'

'Bad news, we're closing.
We can't compete with
the House of Commons'

'Well, that went better than
I was expecting'

Mrs May's deal loses by 230 votes

'Prime Minister, NASA has discovered living beings on Mars and they're all against your Brexit deal'

'This way Mrs May won't
even have to land'

'We've left out a glass of
whisky and a carrot for
Mrs May. That's all she'll get'

Mrs May seeks concessions

'Should we let Mrs May
inside to make her speech?'

'I can take the laughter,
it's the pity I can't bear'

Everyone knows what they don't want

'What do we want least?
When don't we want it?'

'If this ginger biscuit is
a hard Brexit, and this
cup of tea is the
House of Commons …'

'We need a Plan B. I don't mind compromising – but not with people I disagree with'

'To get the title of your own Brexit plan, it's the name of your first pet, followed by your street and then the word "compromise"'

Brexit
Soft & very long

'We're desperate for a second referendum. We sent our Romanian cleaner on the People's Vote march'

'I'm going for a third, and maybe a fourth, Meaningful Drink'

Speaker intervenes

'Of course, you know what
this means, don't you?
No, neither do I'

'Why don't the BBC film
crews in Westminster step in
to stop this Brexit tragedy?'

TV crew save penguins

'The meaningful vote is on March 12. I'm not sure the Labour and Tory parties will still exist by then'

'Forget the Ides of March, the 12th is going to be a complete s***show'

'Whitehall? Go past the
"Nazi Scum" chants, then
straight on till you get to
shouts of "Fascist Liar"'

'You may need to pour
yourself a stiff drink
before I begin'

'I wouldn't go in there, sir,
it's absolutely foul'

'It has just been revealed
that the past two and a half
years have all been a bad
dream that David
Cameron was having'

'And now, once again,
it's Ode to Joy'

Tusk's unfortunate comment

Brexit

'WAIT! I want to ask
you for a third time!'

'Someone should try to limit
the amount of time Mrs May
spends fiddling with her
withdrawal deal'

'*A good guide to what happens next is to ask yourself how this could get any worse*'

'We're not moving the date of Brexit, but we might add an extra 90 days to February'

'I must say, these EU extensions are very moreish'

A further extension looks likely

'Think of it as
a flextension'

'I booked a table with you
at 8pm on the 29th March
to celebrate Brexit. We
might be a bit late ...'

'Remember, whatever
happens, Mrs May is always
having a worse day'

'If Mrs May has taught
us anything, it's that
persevering isn't always
such a good idea'

'Vote Conservative. We're the only party that is really committed to getting rid of Mrs May'

Local elections

Mrs May and Tory Woes

'You know what I miss? Voter apathy'

'Expectation management. Can anyone think of an outcome that is worse than the one we're expecting'

EU elections

Milkshake debacle

'This amazing 16-year-old
girl has come from Sweden
to warn us that the
Tories face extinction'

Mrs May and Tory Woes

'I'm thinking of giving this up to campaign for orderly competent government'

CONSERVATIVE PARTY MEMBERSHIP

'Are you now, or have you ever been, a fruitcake?'

UKIP-ers join Tories

'Spoiler alert. Do you want to know how the Conservative Party ends?'

'The definition of a Theresa May loyalist is someone who thinks she should stay on till next Tuesday'

'If Mrs May promises to leave
Number 10 soon, how can
we be sure she'll pull it off?'

'Which tie says, I'm loyal to
the PM, but if the situation
arose, I could be persuaded
to lead the party?'

'It's been one of those days
for Mrs May'

'We had a whip round
for Theresa May.
Now she owes us £78bn'

Tory Leadership

'BORIS??? RUNNING
FOR TORY LEADER???'

'Have you seen how many
people are standing in the
Tory leadership contest?'

'We're holding Tory leadership candidates here to ease congestion'

'Can I have a selfie? I don't recognise you, so I'm guessing you must be a Tory leadership candidate'

'I'm really only running
to raise my profile and
get a job in the Cabinet'

'Yes, I'll be voting for you
in the leadership contest.
Who is this, by the way?'

'In the next round the
remaining candidates
will have to bake 12
identical chocolate eclairs'

'We've changed the rules.
Leadership candidates must
now have at least eight
undeliverable policies'

Tory Leadership

'Look, it's Rory Stewart on his latest walkabout'

ASCOT

'My horse came last, but it had by far the best social media campaign'

Rory's walkabout causes a stir

'He promised 57 MPs they'd be Chancellor, 43 that they'd be Foreign Secretary ...'

'I just pray the party can now put behind it all that nonsense about unity'

Tory Leadership

'We were called to Jeremy Hunt's property after neighbours heard someone excitedly screaming "I'm going to be Prime Minister"'

'Never mind the backstop. I want Boris to explain how he plans to get red wine stains out of that sofa'

Neighbours report row between Boris and Carrie

'Boris makes model buses.
My hobby is making
detailed, carefully worked
out Brexit plans'

'Is that your plan? If Jeremy
Hunt tries to bring back
fox hunting you'll
prorogue Parliament?'

'Here are the nuclear codes for Boris. And here's a second set of codes for when he loses the first set'

'We've landed in the UK. Brace yourselves, we're expecting turbulence'

Boris wins

'If you can't sleep, maybe you should try adopting an optimistic, can-do attitude'

'Is this the secret plot against Jeremy Corbyn, or the secret plot against Theresa May?'

'I don't know what this means, but Mr Corbyn has dug up all his Jerusalem artichokes'

Labour

Cross-party talks

Alastair Campbell votes Lib Dem

'If you can still feel the pea
under all these mattresses,
Mr Corbyn says you must
never work at the BBC'

Corbyn complains of BBC bias

'My husband's like Chuka
Umunna. After half an hour
he's ready to leave any party'

Chuka leaves Labour
– and Change UK

'Your Majesty, are you
keeping in the line about
the Government not being
able to run a whelk stall?'

'We probably shouldn't light
the candles. You know how
Prince Charles feels about
global warming'

Princess Eugenie's wedding

'It's a Royal Baby Souvenir
Tea Towel'

'And here are some cyanide
pills in case anyone asks
about Archie's godparents'

Harry and Meghan

Royals

'*If you're old enough to remember a time before Brexit, you probably shouldn't still be driving*'

Prince Philip's crash

'And I got this one for my
beautiful brass rubbings
in Salisbury cathedral'

'We've developed a door knob
that can be covered in ten
times as much Novichok'

Russian Spies

'You went to Salisbury
cathedral and you didn't
bring us back a keyring
or a bookmark?'

'We are tourists from Moscow
and we've come to see your
spectacular mountains'

'You have to get out,
Mr President. The banquet
is not a drive-thru'

'Here are the groceries you ordered online. The Chinese government made some substitutions'

'Watch out for the bamboo. We think it's passing sensitive information to the Chinese authorities'

Huawei

'We've narrowed it down. There were only two people at the meeting who can pronounce "Huawei"'

'It's a leaving card from Huawei, Mr Williamson. They knew on Monday that you were going to be sacked'

Drone Airport Chaos

'We don't want a
drone to disrupt any
angels with tidings'

'Only four more sleeps
till we get on a plane'

'Do I have to pay the
Sugar Tax if I'm just going
to throw it over a politician?'

'Waiter, this fly in my soup,
how many calories is it?'

Waitrose Magazine Editor

'I don't eat vegetables
because of the cruel way
Waitrose treats its
magazine editors'

'I'm vegan for environmental
reasons. If sea levels rise,
the moral high ground will
be the only dry bit'

Twitter row

'Will it be done by 2050?
The UK is committed to
zero emissions by then'

'We're not fixing the potholes.
We're just filling them with
all the plastic we don't recycle'

'*And what a lot of non-disclosure agreements you have, Grandma*'

Philip Green

'We've got no local GPs, and I can't Google my symptoms because there's no broadband round here either'

'WAIT! I've just come up with a solution to the Irish backstop'

And finally . . .

Outbreak of horse flu

'It's 4pm. Shall I wake our teenage son to tell him?'

'The Lib Dems are all leaving their conference. Due to passenger numbers we're running fewer trains'

And finally ...

'A bad deal is better
than no deal'

'Hello, technical support?
The chief executive is trying
to leave but the automatic
doors won't open'

Cash machines stop working

'You need to bring down your blood pressure. Avoid doing anything stressful, like trying to book a GP appointment'

'We're advising people to work from home today. One person who took that advice is the driver of the 8.37 to Waterloo…'

And finally...

'I'd call that "highly skilled".
It's a "yes" from me'

'Chips with that?'

Whale in the Thames

'Now Vera Lynn will sing
"There'll Be Scallops Over
The White Cliffs of Dover"'

Scallop wars

'These are the emergency
instructions. If a passenger
starts a racist rant,
pretend to be reading them
and not to notice'

And finally . . .

'I asked for a tea with four sugars. I think you've given me Chateau le Pin Pomerol 2001'

Restaurant mix-up

And finally …

And finally …

'We might need a trade deal
with New Zealand.
For goodness sake don't
beat them'

'The nail-biting cricket final
has inspired a new
generation to take up
drinking and smoking'

England win cricket world cup

'Don't tell them we're British. Pretend we're Mexicans coming to work illegally'

'I'm not a racist, but 50 years ago I told Neil Armstrong to go back where he came from'

And finally …

And finally...

'Well, I've stopped thinking
about Donald Trump's hair'

BBC STARS APOLOGISE
FOR DRUNKEN KISS